LINES from UPSTREAM

SCOTT SCHMIDT
Illustrations by Terri Morgan

www.ten16press.com - Waukesha, WI

Lines from Upstream
Copyrighted © 2020 Scott Schmidt
ISBN 978-1-64538-128-0
Second Edition

Lines from Upstream
by Scott Schmidt

Illustrations by Terri Morgan

All Rights Reserved. Written permission must be secured from the publisher to use or reproduce any part of this book, except for brief quotations in critical reviews or articles.

For information, please contact:

www.ten16press.com
Waukesha, WI

To my Mom,
And my Maria

CONTENTS

A Likely Story.....1

The Catch-All.....4

Mike's Passion....7

Cat Fight.....9

Danny's Wild Ride...15

Mighty Muskie.....19

The Demon Muskie From Hell.....20

The Legend of Todd Franke, Muskie Killer.....26

The Rime of Gus.....29

Two Worms.....34

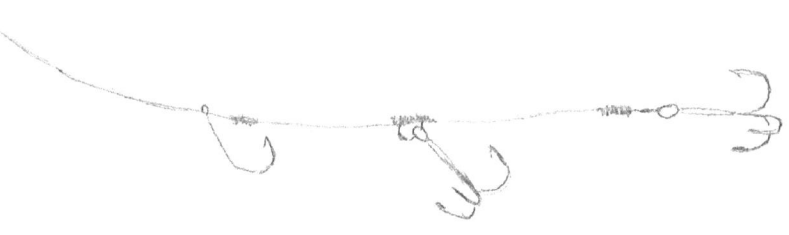

A LIKELY STORY

Outside the Shack it's blizzardy black,
Inside, dimly lit by a lamp.
He's cold and he's wet, frustrated, but yet,
Feels the future is bright at the Camp.

He'll plot and he'll plan where to sit, when to stand,
He knows fresh snow means new tracks,
And these he can trail, through each swamp and swale,
And attempt to turn tracks into Racks.

Nearby, there are shacks with walls full of Racks,
Trophies, that brag of success,
But his walls are bare, no Racks anywhere,
No propensity to impress.

His skills are not lacking when stalking or tracking,
The ways of the woods, no mystery,
But Bucks are not slain and it's hard to explain
Why his Shack has a Rackless wall history.

His shooting excelled when contests were held,
Beer cans and bottles destroyed,
Now it doesn't appear that when shooting at deer
His marksmanship skills are employed.

If you ask the guy why, he'll certainly lie,
He's known for his prevarications,
He'll look in your eyes, make up alibies,
And take pride in his misinformation.

Since the days of his youth he's avoided the Truth,
He will always deny any fault.
So better beware and always prepare
To believe with a big grain of salt.

He'll say maybe one day he'll have Racks on display,
And his walls won't generate scorn.
He talks every year about bagging a deer
With a Rack, for the wall to adorn.

But a leap, unexpected, the Sun's glare, reflected,
For each shot, a new reason for missing.
Consistent bad luck, but each time a Big Buck,
That grows bigger with each reminiscing.

He'll over embellish with obvious relish,
The limits of honesty tested,
Candor ignored, frankness deplored,
And virtue left not unmolested.

The incredible story, his ultimate quarry,
A new lie for every shot taken.
Once the Buck runs away, whatever he'll say,
The Truth will be sorely forsaken.

With space on the wall for Racks, big or small,
His trophies, remarkable stories.
So, if the Buck dies, along with it, the lies,
And all chance for enhanced oratories.

Bucks on the wall stay there for all
To see, they can never be bigger.
Bucks left alive are tales to contrive,
And they grow with each pull of the trigger.

To be honest with you, there's nothing to do
If you want to hear Truth, but keep wishing,
But if you're surprised by his Hunting Shack lies,
Just wait till he talks about Fishing!

Though outside the Shack it's blizzardy black,
Inside, everyone's lit by the fire,
And tales to be spilled over glasses re-filled
Are what make him our favorite liar.

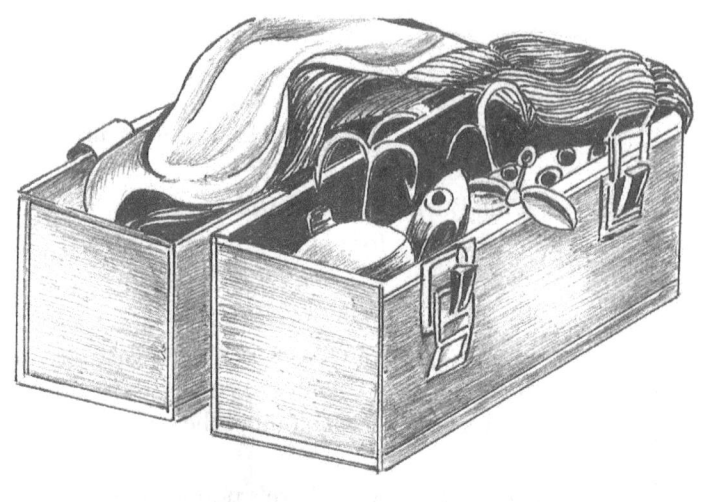

THE CATCH ALL

Vernon found the Catch-All in a rusty little box,
At a yard sale in Price County, underneath a bag of socks.
At first, he didn't believe it, that he could be so blest,
That he'd ever find such treasure Vernon never would have guessed.

A Mighty Lure, the Catch-All, a Legend, passed from old,
With fish catching abilities a wonder to behold,
But many fishing seasons gone, the Catch-All disappeared,
No one knew its whereabouts; its permanent loss was feared.

Until Vernon, by some stroke of luck, or Divine Intervention,
Rediscovered that fabled tool of fishless day prevention.
Staggered, Vernon couldn't believe the magnitude of his luck,
When he paid for the awesome Catch-All and got change back from a buck.

Vernon raced back to his truck and hooked it to his boat,
He snagged his favorite fishing rod, and scrawled his wife a note,
He drove straight to the landing, got the boat into the water,
He motored to a weed bed and got ready for the slaughter.

He tied the Catch-All to his line and rifled out a cast,
A Muskie grabbed the Catch-All, before it even splashed.
Vern let out a joyous cry and fought the Muskie in,
He let it go at boatside, then he casted out again.

The Catch-All hit the water, Vern turned the crank a bit,
The Catch-All barely jiggled, and immediately was hit.
The second fish was bigger but the Catch-All's hooks were strong,
Soon Vern released a Muskie nearly fifty inches long!

And on it went till nearly dawn, Vern hooked, and fought, for sure,
A fish on every single cast with the Magic Catch-All Lure.
Unlike many other anglers, Vernon wasn't one to brag,
Or gab about the lure that had just worn out his drag.

He never used the Catch-All unless he was alone,
Even his beloved wife was never to be shown.
When asked about the secret to his phenomenal success,
Vern was always humble, he'd say, "Just luck, I guess."

Until one day, in a tourney, with the competition tough,
Vern said to me, his partner, "I think I've had enough."
He said, "Put your rod down, Schmidty, you just man the net,
You won't believe this lure I got, we'll win this tourney yet."

Vern reached into his bait box, on his face a silly grin,
Then revealed to me the Catch-All, saying, "Let the fun begin!"
As he held it out to show me, a lump formed in my throat,
For the myth became reality, when a fish jumped in the boat.

Word spread fast across the lake, "The Catch-All has been found!"
The tournament contestants and the judges gathered round.
And soon we were surrounded by a hundred boats, or more,
A chopper hovered overhead, people lined the shore.

The Catch-All worked its Magic, the crowd worked keeping score,
Vern fished till he was tired, then they made him fish some more.
Vernon's arms were getting numb, his line was wearing thin,
But the crowd still hadn't had enough, they made him cast again.

And that was when his line broke, and the Catch-All sailed away,
Through the air in a perfect arc, to everyone's dismay.
At first the crowd was stunned, no sound did we make,
But then, as if on signal, we all jumped in the lake.

I'd never seen such chaos, confusion all around,
Hundreds dived to find the Catch-All; surely some of them could drown.
Boats were swamped as people clawed, and fought with foamy screams,
But they didn't find the Catch-All, that Lure of all our dreams.

When all was peace and calm again, the injuries were many,
Which proved that for the Catch-All, the price they'd pay was any.
A Mighty Lure, the Catch-All, its Magic, and its Charm,
Will cause any type of Angler to risk injury and harm.

Now they say the Legend's over, and the Catch-All's gone for good,
Yet the tale keeps growing taller, just as every Legend should.
They say it's gone forever, to where is anybody's guess,
Just don't ask *me* about the secret to *my* phenomenal success.

MIKE'S PASSION

The shore of the river,
A hot summer night,
Rippled reflections
Of moon, and starlight
Cast a soft luminescence
On a couple, prone,
On the bank, on a blanket,
Together, alone.

It was Mike and his Girl,
And Mike felt he was right,
Conditions were perfect,
That hot summer night.
So, he pulled the girl close,
Whispered soft in her ear,
What he knew, what he wanted,
Desired, sincere.

She responded at once,
Said assertively, "NO!"
But Mike was insistent,
Could not let it go.
The time, the place,
An evening to savor,
The river, the night,
It was all in his favor.

Mike begged and he pleaded,
He argued his case,
But could not his Sweetheart's
Resistance erase.
So, he did what he had to,
He did what it took,
Mike played his best card,
The puppy-dog look.

He looked so pathetic,
How could he not win?
Mike felt his heart soar
When she finally gave in.
Her defenses crumbled,
The girl said, at last,
"OK Mike, go ahead,"
"BUT ONLY ONE CAST!"

CAT FIGHT

In the Forest of Northern Wisconsin,
With the Eagles, Wolves, and Bears,
There once lurked a terrible Tiger,
With scales where there should have been hairs.
For this Tiger wasn't a Feline,
Not your regular dangerous Cat,
She lived in a Lake, underwater,
Where fish kept her long, strong, and fat.
"How could this be?" you might wonder,
"It cannot be true!" you may say,
But listen now to my story,
I say you may think a new way.

It happened in times pre-historic,
A Saber-Tooth swam from the shore
To ravage a huge spawning Muskie,
And the thousands of eggs she bore.
The battle they fought was an epic,
A separate tale to be told,
But finally, when it was over,
The Cat floated silent and cold.
But the essence of Saber-Tooth Tiger
Had infused all the Big Muskie's eggs,
And so came the first Tiger-Muskies,
With fins where there should have been legs.

Each one a natural killer,
Each one an eating machine,
They thrive yet today in Wisconsin,
And each is incredibly mean.
But one reigned over the others,
The biggest and meanest, because
Traits of her father had made her
The most Tiger-like Muskie there was.
She was long, she was sleek and ferocious,
When she moved she glided with grace,
When she opened her jaws, she was frightful,
All teeth where there should have been face.

At the apex of all of predation,
Of a watery realm she was Queen.
She ruled from the top of the food chain,
Over subjects who served as cuisine.
To her, men were merely a nuisance
And they usually wound up the same,
A belly of meat for the Tiger,
For all in her Lake was fair game.
Her Legend spread through the Forest
And brought with it nightmares, and fears
Of the Lake and the Queen of the Tigers
With gills where there should have been ears.

Adventurous men were attracted,
Most foolish, all daring, none wise,
Each, with their lives in the balance,
Would strive for the Tiger's demise.
A few who challenged the Tiger
Would face her and live, others fled,
Most chickened out at the landing,
Some faced her and ended up dead.
The shoreline was littered with wreckage,
Their boats, their equipment, their dreams,
The waves ran red with their battles,
Rosy froth, where there should have been screams.

One day there were rumors reported,
Of a Champion, who might stand a chance!
But what stood out most on arrival was
The dress where there should have been pants.
None had expected a woman,
Not a beauty such as she,
Who exuded game experience,
Confidence, and maturity.
She was long, she was sleek and ferocious,
When she moved she glided with grace,
Her dress was tawny leather,
Trimmed in fur where there should have been lace.

At the apex of all of predation,
Of a Forested realm she was Queen.
She ruled Badgers, Hawks, and Gophers,
Wildcats and Wolverines.
To her, men were merely a nuisance,
And they usually wound up the same,
Disposable, at her convenience,
For sport, any man was fair game.
A Cougar to challenge the Tiger!
A Cat Fight of Epic Proportions!
Who could believe it? Estrogen,
Where there should have been endorphins.

A battle of utmost importance!
A contest of great consequence!
The town filled with gawkers and gamblers,
The atmosphere filled with suspense.
Odds makers at the Casino,
Swamped with bets as the Big Battle neared,
Were unable to point to a favorite,
Dead Even, the odds appeared.
The people poured in from all over,
Campgrounds and resorts became packed,
Much money was spent that eventually went
To the Vault in the Bank, to be stacked.

Finally, the day was upon them,
The Cat-Fight was soon to commence,
The grandstands filled up early,
The anticipation intense.
Concessions were selling like crazy,
Programs and cheap souvenirs,
Bratwurst were selling like hot-cakes,
Business was brisk selling beers.
The Tiger was ready and willing.
The Cougar was limber and stretched.
The Chamber of Commerce was giddy
For the money the Big Cat-Fight fetched.
The Cougar crept down to the water
Where the Tiger was waiting off-shore.
They regarded each other intently,
Uneasy peace, where there should have been war.

The spectators all became silent,
Vendors quit hawking their wares,
Children stopped running and playing,
Gamblers stopped saying their prayers.
With cameras and microphones ready
To record the Historic Event,
The Cougar toe-tested the water,
And that was as far as she went.
Because that's when the Big Alarm sounded.
The one downtown, by the Bank.
A hold-up! The Vault full of money!
The purse for the Fight was to thank.

The Cougar was off in an instant,
The Tiger streaked quick as an arrow,
The Cougar pursued the Robbers,
The Tiger zoomed for the Narrows,
To wait at the bridge on the highway
And ambush those idiot bandits,
To rescue the purse for the Battle.
And it worked out as if they had planned it.
The Robbers were racing the Cougar,
They came to the bridge with their load,
That's where their getaway ended,
Tiger teeth, where there should have been road.

The crooks took one look at their captors
And realized then they were prey.
The last thing they knew? That the wrong thing to do
Was imagine they might get away.
Once the Cougar and Tiger were sated,
They knew they would no longer fight.
After what they had just done together,
To battle now wouldn't feel right.
They laughed, and looked at each other,
Held each other's gaze for some time,
In that moment they each knew the other,
And the feeling they shared was sublime.
Then cops were there, and crowded cars,
A frenzy expecting a brawling,
Instead they saw friends making amends,
Where there should have been maiming and mauling.

Then the Tiger was gone, dove back to the depths,
There are many who say she's still there.
But the Chamber's convinced, she's not been sighted since,
There's no longer need to beware.
The Cougar was hailed as the winner,
Some experts agreed to decry it,
But she turned down the Crown, and before she left town
Said she's leaving out fish from her diet.
She talked of her plans for the future,
How she endeavored to embark
On a quest to the Shore of the Ocean,
To battle the Great Tiger-Shark.

Perhaps one day we'll hear the tales,
How the Cougar's crusade ended,
Or how the Tiger-Muskie's
Disappearance was pretended.
For she'll return, just wait and see,
The Chamber will be sorry,
If she don't, I guess there'll be
An End, where there should have been Story.

DANNY'S WILD RIDE

In early July of the year 2K,
Danny was putting
His tools away.
Chores were done early that fine summer day
And Danny was thinking,
"Work's done, time to play."

It was hot, Dan was sweaty, he felt out of sorts,
So, he changed his long pants
And put on some shorts.
He looked at his legs, all shiny and white,
Like a fat Walleye's belly
In a sock that's too tight.

But comfort was key, Danny thought with a smile,
Who cares what one wears
When he's fishing awhile?
So, with tackle box, rod, and some worms (just in case)
Danny boarded his boat
With a grin on his face.

Now Dan's a big man and his boat's a bit small,
Two benches, an outboard,
But perfect to haul
Dan and his tackle upstream and down,
To fish the deep holes
Where Walleyes abound.

With his hat, which was lucky, and treasured by Dan,
Which he wore, though it made him
A strange looking man,
Pulled tight on his head, the brim flapped in the breeze,
Dan faced the stern, on the bench,
On his knees.

Dan grabbed the starter cord, gave it a tug,
Smoothly it started,
Not even a chug,
So he clambered around, put his rear on the seat,
And headed upstream
For some Walleyes to eat.

The sun on the water, the wind in his face,
Danny twisted the throttle,
The boat motor raced
And shot the craft forward, where the river was wide,
And so began
That Wild Ride.

For then something happened, an occurrence quite rare,
The motor stopped running,
This gave Dan a scare.
"Don't quit on me now," Danny said with a turn,
"There's Walleyes to catch,
And no time to burn."

With a lean and a twist, Danny's hand reached the cord,
He gave it a tug
And the boat motor roared.
It happened so fast there was no time for fear,
Just the realization
He'd left it in gear!

The boat heaved, and pitched Danny over the side,
Where the water was deep
And the river was wide,
And then sped away, leaving Dan in its wake,
Like a big hairy bobber,
Adrift in a lake.

But Dan didn't panic, he was too cool for that,
The first thing he did
Was rescue his hat.
Then he watched as his boat slowed and leaned in an arc,
And he started to swim
Toward a spot that he marked.

For he knew if the boat circled back within reach,
He could grab on the side
And cling like a leech.
Danny swam to the spot, treaded water a bit,
The boat puttered closer,
This would be it!

Danny lunged upward and managed a grip
But his hands were all wet
And they started to slip,
So, from deep down inside, Danny summoned such power,
He clamped down so hard
He hung on for an hour.

Danny's boat's made of metal but it's been noted since,
He clamped down so tightly
He left fingerprints.
Danny held tight with that strength that he'd found,
While his boat kept on circling,
Around and around.

Until a couple of guys who were fishing that day,
Rescued our hero
And sent him away.
And to Dan's parting "Thank You's!" they grinned and replied,
"That must have been
Some Wild Ride!"

MIGHTY MUSKIE

Mighty Muskie, reigning deep
Safe in your aquatic keep
Lord of all that swim or creep
Past weed beds green and drop-offs steep
You live
Suspended over rock and weed
Nature's bounty for your feed
Killing not for lust or greed
Killing only what you need
To live
A life not easy, though you're strong
And wise enough to get along
In the element where you belong
Where Might is right and Weak is wrong

THE DEMON MUSKIE FROM HELL

On the calm summer evening
Of a hot sultry day,
I stood on the shore
And I watched a boy play.
He threw out a stick
For his dog in the water,
The dog went to fetch
And that's when he bought'er.
Foam and spray flew,
The water it churned,
The dog disappeared
And never returned.
I stood there in shock
While the boy cried so hard;
He'd lost his best friend,
His old Saint Bernard.
And that's how it started,
This tale I must tell,
Of The Demon
Muskie
From Hell.

In a tavern that night
I described the event.
They listened at first,
Then away they all went
To laugh and to snicker
At one such as I,
Who'd thought they'd believe
Such an obvious lie.
They said I was crazy,
Deluded, I think,
Once friendly, bartenders
Stopped serving me drinks.
So, I took myself home
And mentioned no more
That little boy's dog
Not reaching the shore.
Yet I was certain,
It made my blood gel,
Our lake now belonged to
The Demon
Muskie
From Hell.

Within weeks, frogs and ducks
Disappeared from the lake,
When anglers went out
Not a catch could they make.
Our beautiful lake,
So clear and spring fed,
Turned mysteriously murky,
With waves tinted red.
When a DNR shocking crew
Went out one night,
Their survey results
Caused a terrible fright.
The whole town was stunned
When the DNR said
That our lake was now totally,
Hopelessly dead.
Yet only two people,
That young boy and I,
Knew for a fact
What had caused it to die,
For he knew as I did
That in our lake dwelled
A horrible monster;
The Demon
Muskie
From Hell.

Then rumors started,
And gossip galore,
A man lost a bull
That was grazing on shore.
They said a young couple,
Alone on the beach,
Heard a commotion
And a horrible screech.
What they claimed to have seen
No one believed, of course,
(I mean, who'd think a Muskie
Could eat a whole horse?)
But I knew they weren't lying,
As did my young friend,
And together we planned
To capture and end
The life of that monster
And his terrible spell.
Together, we'd kill
The Demon
Muskie
From Hell.

So, we readied our tackle
And sharpened our hooks.
But when folks saw us fishing
They gave us such looks,
Some said we were stupid,
Some said we were dumb,
All laughed at our folly
When they saw our boat come.
But we kept on fishing,
We knew what was there,
As for what the town thought,
Well, we just didn't care.
And finally, it happened,
One wet, windy day,
We sighted the Demon,
Some distance away.
We just hadn't figured,
We'd failed to foretell,
That *we'd be* the prey of
The Demon
Muskie
From Hell.

He was charging our boat,
His jaws opened wide,
Too late to run,
We had no place to hide.
His teeth were like butcher knives,
Eyes bloody red,
A great grey-green tail
Propelled him ahead.
He rammed us head-on
And he bit out a chunk
Of our little boat's bottom,
I knew we were sunk.
As he circled the boat,
We watched him with dread,
I had to do something
Or else we'd be dead,
So I grabbed up an oar
And when he swam by,
I swung at his head
And it stuck in his eye.
I jammed it in hard
With a turn and a twist,
The Muskie lunged for me,
I was lucky, he missed.
Then his tail struck the boat
And over we fell,
Into the lake with
The Demon
Muskie
From Hell.

My friend was a swimmer
But not so was I,
As I started to sink
I felt something brush by.
In a panic, I reached out
And tried to grab hold,
It was thick as a tree trunk,
And slimy, and cold,
But I wrapped my arms round it,
Squeezed with all of my might,
And I didn't let go
Until shore was in sight.
Then we fought through the shallows,
And up to the shore,
And although I made it,
I was bloody, and sore,
And the last thing I knew
Was how good dry land feels
With an aquatic Demon
Hard on your heels.
Then I passed out,
Forward I fell,
Amazed I'd escaped from
The Demon
Muskie
From Hell.

When I finally came to,
My mind was a blank.
I went straight to the tavern,
And sat there,
And drank.
But now, twenty years later,
I'm quitting the booze.
Our lake is now famous,
Our town's in the news.
The Demon is dead!
The curse has been lifted!
He hangs on the wall
Of a fisherman gifted
With drive and courage
And the skill that it took
To subdue such a Monster
With rod and with hook.
He'd spent his whole life out there,
Fishing alone;
Trolling and casting,
Tired to the bone,
And when asked by reporters
What drove him so hard,
Said, "That Devil ate
My Saint Bernard!"
And so ends my story,
This tale I must tell,
Of The Demon
Muskie
From Hell.

THE LEGEND OF TODD FRANKE, MUSKIE KILLER

Todd Franke loved to catch Muskies
He'd fish for them every day
He kept all he caught for his supper
He never let one get away

The Price County Muskies would tremble
At the mention of Todd Franke's name
They decided to look for a Champion
Who could beat Franke at his own game

Word spread fast through Wisconsin
Minnesota, and Canada too
They needed a heroic Muskie
No average Muskie would do

And they came from all over the country
The St. Lawrence and every Great Lake
But none was a match for Todd Franke
He left them all dead in his wake

Until a Lunker from up in the Flowage
Decided enough was enough
To him, those who'd failed were mere minnows
Todd Franke could not be that tough

He headed downstream through the River
Up Butternut Creek, to the Lake
There he would challenge Todd Franke
The pride of all Muskies at stake

He wasn't to be disappointed
Todd Franke soon drifted in sight
The Big Muskie followed Todd's bucktail
Till the moment to strike was just right

When Todd saw that Big Muskie follow
He couldn't believe his good luck
Until his bucktail was reeled to the boat side
Because that's when the Big Muskie struck

The Muskie came out of the water
And landed with Todd, in the boat
Todd frantically tried to avoid him, but
The Muskie went right for his throat

Then they slugged it out by the live-well
They grappled around in the stern
Then up to the bow where they wrestled
But neither advantage could earn

Some folks say they fought for an hour
Some folks say they fought for a day
Some folks say they battled much longer
Who was winning? No one could say

Both the Muskie and Todd were exhausted
But neither for mercy would beg
And when Todd dropped his guard for a moment
The Big Muskie bit down on his leg

That's when Todd knew he was losing
And the Muskie knew Todd's strength was spent
So he chomped one more time on Todd's ankle
And back to the water he went

The Price County Muskies were angry
"Todd Franke's not dead!" they complained
But the Big Muskie said not to worry
"I accomplished my goal" he explained

And the next time Todd Franke went fishing
The Muskies all saw what he meant
For they noticed this one striking difference
No dead Muskies wherever Todd went

So the Hero returned to the Flowage
And the Price County Muskies knew peace
For Todd Franke had learned a Great Lesson
The value of Catch and Release

Todd Franke still loves to catch Muskies
But he lets them all go now, they say
For the scars on his leg still remind him how
The Big One let Todd get away

THE RIME OF GUS

Old Gus retired from the Mill
With one thing on his mind,
To fish for Muskies every day
And catch all he could find.

In Gus's dreams there was a Fish
As long as Gus was tall,
Old Gus was sure that someday soon
He'd have it on the wall.

Every day his hopes were high,
His heart filled with elation,
But every night it was the same,
Gus only felt frustration.

He fished the weeds, he fished the rocks,
He fished the deepest spots,
He put his time in on the lakes,
But lucky? Gus was not.

One day Old Gus found a spot
Way back in on the Flowage.
No one ever fished that place,
Not to Gus's knowledge.

Weedy, deep, and full of rocks,
The perfect place, it seemed,
Old Gus had finally found the home
Of the Muskie of his dreams.

The sky was dark, the air was warm,
The wind a wee bit strong,
So Gus tied on his favorite lure,
A Bucktail, black and long.

Gus's rod was new and stout,
Graphite, long and light,
His line was super heavy,
And his drag was set just right.

He packed his cheek with a fresher chew,
And spit some on his bait,
Then casted near some sunken weeds,
He didn't have long to wait.

Behind his lure Gus spied a shape
Some five or six feet long,
Old Gus just kept on reeling,
Prayed nothing would go wrong.

The Bucktail blade spun perfectly,
Vibrating, flashed attraction,
Gus swung the rod tip left to right,
For a little extra action.

The cast was done, the line reeled in,
The Muskie was too late,
But Old Gus knew a trick or two;
He did a figure-eight.

The Muskie hit next to the boat,
Gus shuddered at its size!
Gus was amazed, there had to be
A foot between its eyes!

Gus set the hooks. The fight was on!
The Fish gave a mighty pull,
Gus held on as the line screamed out,
He knew his hands were full.

The Monster thrashed next to the boat,
And gave Old Gus a soaking.
Gus was glad his reel got wet,
It kept the thing from smoking.

He thought of clubbing the Muskie then,
But just knew it wouldn't work.
The Muskie looked Gus in the eye,
Gus gave another jerk.

The Muskie turned, it jumped, and rolled,
Its strength caused Gus to wonder,
Old Gus focused on the fight,
Oblivious to the thunder.

The Muskie pulled the boat
At least a half a mile, or more,
The battle raged across the Flowage,
A long, long way from shore.

Gus's arms were getting weak,
The Muskie dived and swirled,
He knew he had to catch that Fish,
It was the Biggest in the World!

An hour after his fateful cast,
The battle was nearly done.
The Muskie made a last-ditch pull,
And Gus knew he had won.

His mind was all aflood with thoughts
Of newspapers and TV,
This massive Fish would bring Gus fame,
It was plain to see.

With ready gaff in his right hand,
The left with rod tip high,
Poor Gus never expected
The Lightning from the sky.

That awesome bolt stopped Gus's heart.
It shocked the Muskie dead.
They found them both, in the Flowage,
Floating, head to head.

Gus's funeral was unique,
But everybody knew
That what they'd done was just the thing
Old Gus would want them to.

They buried Gus and the Muskie together,
The epitaph goes like this:
**HERE LIES A MAN
WITH NO REGRETS
HE DIED WHILE CATCHING FISH**

TWO WORMS

Two worms in a bed
Met and one said,
"How would I look
On a fisherman's hook?"
His friend sighed
Quite disjointedly,
And replied,
Somewhat pointedly,
"I think
you'd most likely
look dead."

THE END

ABOUT THE AUTHOR AND ILLUSTRATOR

Scott Schmidt and Terri Morgan
both live and work in Northern
Wisconsin. This is their first book
they have created together and
look forward to publishing more in
the near future.

www.ingramcontent.com/pod-product-compliance
Lightning Source LLC
Chambersburg PA
CBHW071412160426
42813CB00085B/1077